PICTURESQUE
NORTH COUNTRY

Compiled by Frank Graham
From Old Prints

FRANK GRAHAM
6 Queen's Terrace, Newcastle upon Tyne, 2

Published 1968

© 900409 12 6

Printed in Great Britain by Northumberland Press Ltd, Gateshead
Bound by Richard Clay (The Chaucer Press) Ltd, Bungay, Suffolk

FOREWORD

Our book of old prints called *Northumberland and Durham 100 Years Ago* was so well received that we have now published a second volume. Many towns not covered in the first volume are here represented. We have also used some larger views, many of them exceedingly rare, but have avoided views which would need reducing in size so much that their quality would be affected.

Many of the prints are book plates which can be found in various local histories. The four views of Berwick are from the *History of Berwick upon Tweed* by John Fuller, 1799 and the two coal mines are from T. H. Hair's *Sketches of the Coal Mines in Northumberland and Durham*. The well known local artist J. W. Carmichael has contributed a number of Newcastle and Tyne views from the two books *Architectural and Picturesque Views in Newcastle upon Tyne*, published in 1842, and *Views on the Tyne*, first issued in 1828 but re-published many years later.

The large drawings of Bamburgh, Dunstanburgh and Durham Castle Gateway are by T. M. Richardson. They were drawn early in the nineteenth century but were first published in 1881 in a large volume called *Antiquities of the Border Counties*. A number of the market illustrations are from *Views of the County Palatine of Durham* by E. Mackenzie and M. Ross, 1834. We have also used Mackenzie's *Descriptive and Historical Account of Newcastle upon Tyne*, 1827, for two of the Newcastle views.

Six of the large castle drawings are by Thomas Hearne and are from his famous book, *Antiquities of Great Britain*, published in the eighteenth century. In the present volume are many illustrations of Alnwick and Warkworth Castles. They are taken from a book called *Castles of Alnwick and Warkworth*. From sketches by C. F. Duchess of Northumberland. They were drawn on stone by J. D. Harding whose name is attached to the views in the List of Plates.

The remaining views are from a variety of sources, three of the fine, and rare, prints of Darlington having been produced locally. Most of the prints have been reproduced in the same size as the originals, but a few have been slightly reduced.

The last plate in the book is a representation of the Tyne God, taken from John Brand's *History and Antiquities of the Town and County of Newcastle upon Tyne*, published in 1789. We now use this historic drawing as the emblem of our publishing house.

LIST OF PLATES

St NICHOLAS CHURCH.

GREYS MONUMENT.

PUBLISHED BY W.H.LIZARS, EDIN^R

Drawn by J. W. Carmichael.

Engraved by Lambert & Collard.

NEWCASTLE.

NEWCASTLE-UPON-TYNE FROM THE SOUTH.

Drawn by J.W.Carmichael.   Published by W. & T. Fordyce, Newcastle.   Engraved by W. Collard.

EXCHANGE, SANDHILL.

Drawn by J.W.Carmichael.   Published by W. & T. Fordyce, Newcastle.   Engraved by W. Collard.

GRAINGER STREET.

Drawn by T.M. Richardson.   Published by W. & T. Fordyce, Newcastle.   Engraved by W. Collard.

THE SIDE.

Drawn by T. Allom.   Published by W. & T. Fordyce, Newcastle.   Engraved by J. Sands.

ST. NICHOLAS CHURCH.

GREY MONUMENT.

Drawn by T. Allom.   Published by W. & T. Fordyce, Newcastle.   Engraved by W. Miller.

ALL SAINTS' CHURCH

Drawn by T. M. Richardson.   Published by W. & T. Fordyce, Newcastle.   Engraved by H. Collard.

11

ELDON SQUARE.

Drawn by W. Westall A.R.A.   E. Finden sculp.

NEWCASTLE.

FROM WESTGATE HILL.

Drawn by T.M. Richardson.   Published by W. & T. Fordyce, Newcastle.   Engraved by W. Collard.

WESTGATE STREET.

Drawn by J.W.Carmichael   Published by W.&T.Fordyce,Newcastle.   Engraved by W.Collard

OUSEBURN VIADUCT.

Drawn by J.W.Carmichael   Engraved by Lambert & Collard

WALKER QUAY.

From the West.

14

Drawn by W Boosey

Published by Andrew Reid, 117 Pilgrim St. Newcastle-on-Tyne.

GREY STREET, NEWCASTLE.

CENTRAL RAILWAY STATION, NEWCASTLE.

THE ASSEMBLY ROOMS,
Opened June 24. 1776.

Hawkins sculp.

The BLACK FRIARS, at NEWCASTLE, in Northumberland.

MICHAELMAS MONDAY.

KEELMEN'S HOSPITAL & PROCESSION.

18

GATESHEAD.

from the Quayside.

S?. MARY'S CHURCH GATESHEAD.

To the Right Worshipful. John Erasmus Blackett. Esq.r Mayor of Newcastle upon Tyne,

This VIEW of the RUINS of the BRIDGE of that TOWN:

as they appeared after the Fall thereof in November 1771.

Is most respectfully Inscribed, by his very obliged and most devoted, faithful Servant, John Bruno

October 27.th 1772

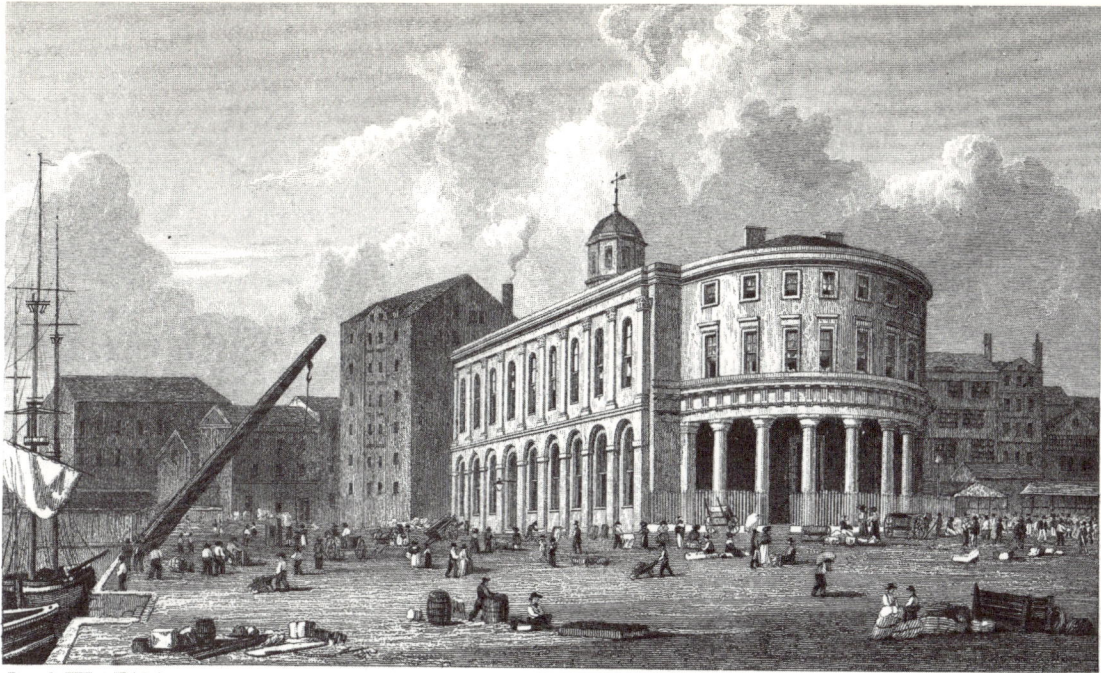

GUILD-HALL OR EXCHANGE, NEWCASTLE ON TYNE.

SCOTSWOOD BRIDGE, OVER THE TYNE.

21

THE MONASTRY OF GREY FRIARS, NEWCASTE UPON TYNE;

NOW THE RESIDENCE OF MAJOR ANDERSON,

To whom this view is gratefully inscribed by   The Publishers.

22

WESTGATE, NEWCASTLE

Drawn by B. Green.

On Stone by J. Sager.

NEW CORN EXCHANGE, &c.

To be erected opposite St. Nicholas Church, NEWCASTLE upon TYNE.

S.O. WILKINSON & SON   MATTHEW WILSON

Drawn by I.W.Carmichael

Engraved by Lambert & Collard

ASCENSION DAY.

T. Allom.

J. Sands.

LEMINGTON IRON WORKS, ON THE TYNE.

BRINKBURN PRIORY.

Printed and Published by W. Davison, Alnwick.

CRASTER HOUSE,

The Seat of Shafto Craster, Esqr.

Printed and Published by W. Davison, Alnwick.

DILSTON CASTLE,

Formerly the Seat of the Unfortunate James Earl of Derwent-water.

Taken 1st April 1822.

Printed and Published by W. Davison, Alnwick.

27

ROCK HOUSE,

FROM THE SOUTH. NORTH.

The Seat of C. Bosanquet Esq.

Published April 1826 by W. Davison, Alnwick.

DRAWN & ENGRAVED BY J LEITCH, GLASGOW.

FROM A SKETCH BY J WELCH F.S.A.

28

Jn.º Karr sculp.

TWIZELL BRIDGE AND CASTLE,

Printed and Published by W. Davison Alnwick.

Drawn & Etched by T. M. Richardson

Aquatinted by T. Sutherland

DUNSTANBOROUGH CASTLE, NORTHUMBERLAND, AFTER A STORM.

DUNSTANBURGH CASTLE

From the South West

Printed and Published by W. Davison, Alnwick.

ALNWICK CASTLE IN ITS ANCIENT STATE,

From the North-East.

Engraved by Jas Byrn, from an Original Painting.

Printed and Published by W. Davison, Alnwick.

Drawn & Etched by T. M. Richardson.

THE BARBICAN, ALNWICK CASTLE.

Engraved by D. Havell.
16 Howard Street, Strand.

33

THE SECOND GATEWAY AND THE ENTRANCE TO THE KEEP.

EAST VIEW OF ALNWICK CASTLE.

ALNWICK CASTLE.

Drawn on Stone by J.P. Harding made copied on a Reduced Scale, from an Old Picture.

Printed by C. Hullmandel

DRAWN BY W. HALL.

ENGRAVED BY J. KERR.

ALNWICK CHURCH FROM THE SOUTH EAST.

Printed and Published by W. Davison, Alnwick.

T. Allom. M. J. Starling.

ALNWICK ABBEY, NORTHUMBERLAND.

Drawn by W. Westall, A.R.A. Engraved by Edw.ᵈ Finden.

BAMBRO CASTLE.

Drawn & Etched by T. M. Richardson

Repainted by T. Sutherland

BAMBOROUGH CASTLE, NORTHUMBERLAND, Storm coming on.

Engraved by Jeavons from a Drawing by W. Weber for the Border Antiquities of England & Scotland.

BAMBOROUGH CASTLE.

FERN ISLANDS,

From the East.

Printed and Published by W. Davison, Alnwick.

Drawn by T. H. Nicholson.

THE CHURCH PIT, WALLSEND.

Drawn by T.Hearne.

Engraved by W.Byrne & T.Medland.

To the Right Honourable Hugh Baron Percy, &c. &c.
this View of WARKWORTH CASTLE is inscribed
By his Lordship's most obedient Servants, the Hearne & W.m Byrne.

Drawn on Stone by J.D.Harding, exactly copied on a reduced Scale, from an Old Picture

WARKWORTH CASTLE.

Printed by C.Hullmandel

43

Drawn on Stone by J.D.Harding.

Printed by C.Hullmandel.

N. VIEW OF WARKWORTH CASTLE.

Engraved by J.Walker from an Original Drawing by Girtin.

Publish'd May 1.1799 by J.Walker No.16, Rosomans Street, London.

WARKWORTH.

44

Drawn on Stone by J B Harding Printed by C Hullmandel

THE LION TOWER AND CRADYFARGUS, WARKWORTH CASTLE.

Drawn on Stone by J B Harding Printed by C Hullmandel

GATE HOUSE OF WARKWORTH CASTLE.
Interior View.

Drawn by J. M. W. Turner R.A.

Engraved by W. Tombleson.

Holy Island
Northumberland.

London, Published May 1835 for the Proprietor by Robert Jennings & William Tegg, Cheapside.

LINDISFARNE PRIORY.

INTERIOR LOOKING EAST.

Durham: Published by George Andrews & R.W. Billings. October 1845.

Drawn by T.Hearne

Engraved by W.Byrne

To the Hon.ble Sir Ralph Payne, Knight Companion of the most honourable Order of the Bath

This View of the MONASTERY at TYNEMOUTH is Inscribed

By his most obedient Servants ~ Thomas Hearne and William Byrne

London. Published as the Act directs 1.June 1784 by W Byrne &T.Hearne.

To the Right Hon.ble The Earl of Carlisle, Viscount Howard of Morpeth, &c.&c.&c.

This View of MORPETH CASTLE is inscribed

By His Lordship's most obedient Servants, Thomas Hearne & William Byrne.

London, Published Oct. 2, 1784, by T.Hearne & W.Byrne.

49

HESLEYSIDE,
NORTHUMBERLAND.

Drawn by J.P.Neale.   Engraved by W. Radclyffe.

CAPHEATON,
NORTHUMBERLAND.

ROTHBURY CHURCH.
North.ᵈ
Published August 1, 1823. by W. Davison Alnwick.

BAMBURGH CHURCH.
North.ᵈ
Published April 14, 1823. by W. Davison Alnwick.

MITFORD CHURCH
North.ᵈ
Published 1 April 1824. by W. Davison Alnwick.

ST ANDREWS CHURCH BYWELL,
North.ᵈ
Published 1 Nov.ʳ 1824. by W. Davison Alnwick.

RYTON CHURCH.
C.ᵗʸ of Durham
Published May 1830. by W. Davison Alnwick.

WOOLER CHURCH,
North.ᵈ
Published 1 Oct.ʳ 1823. by W. Davison Alnwick.

BYWELL HALL,

NORTHUMBERLAND

The Seat of J. W. Beaumont Esq. M.P.

Published August 1830, by W. Davison Alnwick.

VIEW *of the* TOWN HALL *from the Head of* HIDE HILL.

VIEW *of* BERWICK CHURCH

Drawn by A. Carse. Engraved by R. Scott.

INSIDE VIEW OF BERWICK BARRACKS.

Drawn by Joseph Alexander, Berwick. Engraved by R. Scott.

VIEW *of the* BARRACKS *and* PARADE *from the* WALLS *above the* COW PORT.

Drawn by J W Carmichael   Engraved by Lambert & Collard

NORTH SHIELDS.

Drawn by J W Carmichael   Engraved by Lambert & Collard

CARVILLE SHORE

MERTOUN ABBEY CHURCH.

Engraved by Nivis, from a Painting by L. Clennell, for the Border Antiquities of England & Scotland.

THE DEPOT, HEXHAM

57

TYNEMOUTH CASTLE.

Wreck of the Betsy Cairns 18 Feb. 1827. This Vessel brought to England William 3d in 1688.

TYNEMOUTH PRIORY.

Etched by W. Collard.

MARKET PLACE SOUTH SHIELDS.

SEAHAM HARBOUR.

FROM THE SOUTH EAST.

Drawn by T. Hearne F.S.A.

London. Published as the Act directs. June 1. 1793. by W. Byrne. Nº 79. Titchfield Street.

Engraved by W. Byrne.

To John Holland, Esqr. of Ford, Derbyshire,
This View of BARNARD CASTLE, is Inscribed
By his most obedient humble Servant William Byrne.

Wallard Sculp.

MARKET PLACE, STOCKTON.

HARTLEPOOL.

J. Archer Sculpt

Drawn by R. W. Billings.

EVLANTON CHURCH.

Engraved by Geo. Winter.

J. C. NAPIER DEL & LITH.

VIEW OF ST CUTHBERT'S CHURCH DARLINGTON,

TAKEN FROM THE MARKET PLACE.

This Church is supposed to have been built by the Great and Powerful Prelate HUGH PUDSEY in the 12th Century the Foundation
Charter being lost leaves the History of the Church in darkness The elegant Spire was struck by Lightning on Tuesday the 17th July 1750 and
was so shattered as to render it necessary to have the upper part of it taken down in rebuilding it several of the old Ornaments were omitted
the rells at the angles &c which deprive it of much beauty

VIEW OF THE MARKET PLACE, DARLINGTON

Printed and Published by Wm Oliver Market Place, Darlington Decr 1843.

TAKEN FROM THE TALBOT INN, HIGHROW

Deerhouse in the Park, Bishop's Auckland, Durham.

Pub. by Joseph Hollis.

Bishop's Auckland, Durham.

Pub. by Joseph Hollis.

Bridge & Viaduct, Bishop's Auckland, Durham.

Pub. by Joseph Hollis.

Palace, Bishop's Auckland, Durham.

Pub. by Joseph Hollis.

Hurworth on the Tees.

Pub by Rapp & Dresser, Darlington.

Neasham Hall, on the Tees.

Pub by Rapp & Dresser, Darlington.

69

Drawn by T.Hearne. from a Sketch by E.Edwards.

Engraved by W.Byrne.

To John Tempest Esqr. Member of Parliament for the City of Durham,
This View of BRANCEPETH CASTLE is Inscribed
By his most obedient Servants William Byrne, and Thomas Hearne

London Published as the Act directs, 1 Feb. 1782, by T.Hearne & W.Byrne.

Drawn by T.Hearne

The Figures by F. Bartolozzi

Engrav'd by W.Byrne & S.Middiman

To the Right Hon.ble Richard Lumley Saunderson Earl of Scarborough
Viscount & Baron Lumley, &c. this View of LUMLEY CASTLE, is Inscribed By His LORDSHIP's
most obedient Servants, Thomas Hearne and William Byrne

London: Published as the Act directs 1 Jan 1779 by T.Hearne & W.Byrne.

HETTON COLLIERY.

Drawn by T. H. Weir. Etched by J. Brown.

Etched by J.Archer.

SUNDERLAND,
From the North Pier.

FRAMWELLGATE, DURHAM.

Drawn & Etched by Pearson.

Drawn by W. Westall A.R.A.   Engraved by ... Francis.

ELVET BRIDGE, DURHAM.

T. Allom.   J. Redaway.

THE GALILEE, WEST END OF DURHAM CATHEDRAL.

Drawn & Etched by T.M.Richardson.

GATEWAY, DURHAM CASTLE, Demolished in 1818.

EYRE-BRIDGE, DERBAN.

Drawn by R. Billings.

Engraved by G.B. Smith.

THE NORTH SIDE OF DURHAM CATHEDRAL.

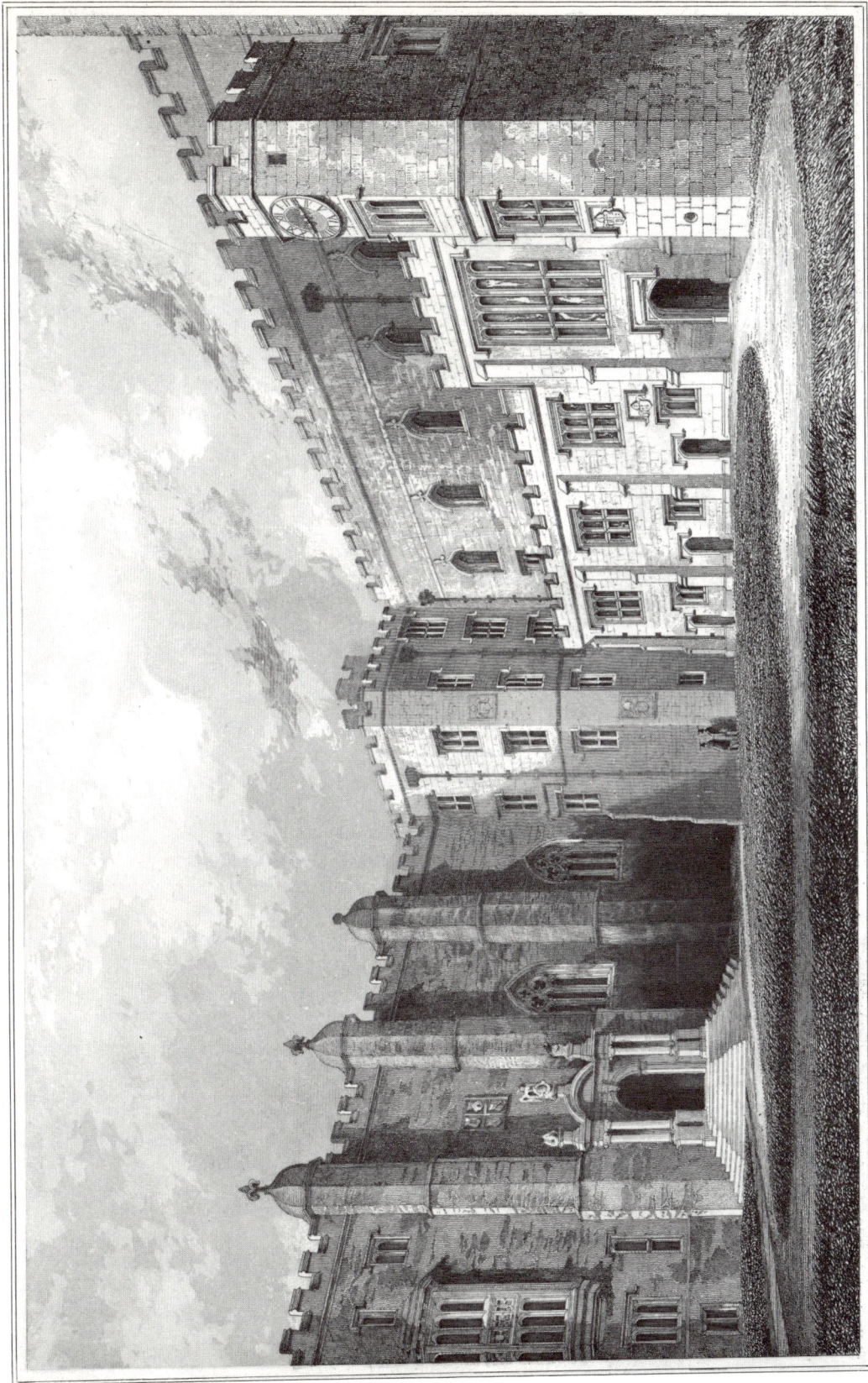

Drawn by R.W. Billings.

Engraved by George Winter.

THE GRAND FRONT OF LUMLEY CASTLE.

Designed by Sir Wm. Chambers.

J. Fittler Sculp.